# Mighty Fun Activities for Practising Times Tables, Book 2

## 3, 4, 6 and 8 Times Tables

Hannah Allum
Hannah Smart

Brilliant
PUBLICATIONS

We hope you and your pupils enjoy the activities in this book. Brilliant Publications publishes many other books for use in primary schools. To find out more details on any of the titles listed below, please log onto our website: www.brilliantpublications.co.uk.

**Other titles in the Mighty Fun Activities for Practising Times Tables series**
Book 1: 2, 5 and 10 times tables                                      978-1-78317-267-2
Book 3: 7, 9, 11 and 12 times tables                                  978-1-78317-269-6

**By the same authors**
The Mighty Multiples Times Table Challenge                            978-0-85747-629-6

**Other maths titles**
Deck Ahoy! Primary Maths Activities Using Just a Deck of Cards        978-1-78317-178-1

Maths Problem Solving, Year 1                                         978-1-903853-74-0
Maths Problem Solving, Year 2                                         978-1-903853-75-7
Maths Problem Solving, Year 3                                         978-1-903853-76-4
Maths Problem Solving, Year 4                                         978-1-903853-77-1
Maths Problem Solving, Year 5                                         978-1-903853-78-8
Maths Problem Solving, Year 6                                         978-1-903853-79-5

Maths Problems and Investigations, Years 1–2                         978-0-85747-626-5
Maths Problems and Investigations, Years 3–4                         978-0-85747-627-2
Maths Problems and Investigations, Years 5–6                         978-0-85747-628-9

Open-ended Maths Investigations, Years 1–2                           978-1-78317-184-2
Open-ended Maths Investigations, Years 3–4                           978-1-78317-185-9
Open-ended Maths Investigations, Years 5–6                           978-1-78317-186-6

Sum Fun Maths Assessment, Years 1–2                                  978-1-78317-083-8
Sum Fun Maths Assessment, Years 3–4                                  978-1-78317-084-5
Sum Fun Maths Assessment, Years 5–6                                  978-1-78317-085-2

Published by Brilliant Publications Limited
Unit 10
Sparrow Hall Farm
Edlesborough
Dunstable
Bedfordshire
LU6 2ES, UK

Website:     www.brilliantpublications.co.uk
Tel:         01525 222292

The name Brilliant Publications and the logo are registered trademarks.

Written by Hannah Allum and Hannah Smart
Illustrated by Gaynor Berry
Cover by Brilliant Publications Limited and Gaynor Berry

© Text Hannah Allum and Hannah Smart 2016
© Design Brilliant Publications 2016

Printed ISBN:   978-1-78317-268-9
ebook ISBN:    978-1-78317-272-6

First printed and published in the UK in 2016.

The right of  Hannah Allum and Hannah Smart to be identified as the author of this work has been asserted by themselves in accordance with the Copyright, Designs and Patents Act 1988.

# Contents

# Introduction

The *Mighty Fun Activities for Practising Times Tables* series uses superheroes to motivate children to practise all of the skills needed to solve multiplication, division and word based times table problems. Superheroes appeal to even the most reluctant of learners and instil a positive and competitive attitude towards learning. The aim is for children to become excited and motivated enough to want to learn and practise their times tables.

The mighty superheroes are based upon the sporty characters in our highly popular whole-school reward-based scheme, *The Mighty Multiples Times Table Challenge*. The sheets in this book can be used in conjunction with the series or independently.

There are three books in the *Mighty Fun Activities for Practising Times Tables* series:
Book 1:      2, 5 and 10 times tables
Book 2:      3, 4, 6 and 8 times tables
Book 3:      7, 9, 11 and 12 times tables

The books contain reproducible sheets and are designed to be used as flexible teaching aids which teachers can dip in and out of in any order to support the learning of any times table. They work equally well as stand alone 5 to 20 minute lesson reinforcements or as regular times table learning.

We recognise that all children learn in different ways and that they need to have opportunities to apply their knowledge and skills. For each times table there is a mixture of practical activities to develop their understanding and written activities to consolidate their knowledge.

There is also an exciting wrist watch and mask for each times table for children to make and wear. These can be used as an introduction to each character or to consolidate learning. Children will become mightily good at their times tables by using their mighty powers! Looking at their watch or mask is a fun and exciting way to memorise the times tables.

The mixed times table sheets at the back of the book allow children to apply the skills gained in learning individual tables, working out for themselves which multiple facts and methods they need to use.

The answers to the code sheets are given on page 65.

# A quick introduction to the sheets

Approximate time needed to complete the main activity on the sheet. The time can be altered to suit individuals or groups of children who require more or less time. Children will enjoy the challenge of beating **Dennis the Demon Digit Demolisher** and will feel a sense of pride and achievement if they can successfully beat the super villain.

Times table covered by sheet is clearly stated.

Children can self-assess how well they feel they have done by colouring in the circles:
1 circle = I need a bit of help please.
2 circles = I'm getting there.
3 circles = I've got it!

Read the instructions aloud if necessary so that pupils are clear what they have to do.

### Water SOS!

15:00  4x

How did you do?

*Lorraine the Loathsome Dragon* has breathed holes into the side of the pool so the water is draining out! The only way to save the day is to pour 4x as much water into the pool as quickly as possible! Turn on all the taps by multiplying the numbers on the taps by 4.

7  9  5
3  8  11
6  10  2
12  4  0

#### Home Challenge
Time how long your bath takes to fill. Can you multiply the number of minutes by 4? Can you time how long it takes other things to fill? Your sink? A can? A bucket? Times the numbers by 4!

#### Mighty Challenge
Can you see any numbers around you in your class? Can you multiply them by 4 and then by 4 again?

The Home Challenges provide practical and physical learning activities that can be assigned as homework. They have been designed to encourage parents to join in as their children develop their times table knowledge at home in an active way.

The Mighty Challenges allow children to self-extend and apply the skills which have been targeted during the activity even further.

# Meet the mighty sporty superheroes!

In this book you will meet four mighty sporty superheroes (and some of their friends):

**Mighty
Hypersonic
Heather**
The 3x Table
Champion!

**Mighty
Fishtail
Freda**
The 4x Table
Champion!

**Mighty
Bubble Bursting
Brenda**
The 6x Table
Champion!

**Mighty
Time Traveller
Tracey**
The 8x Table
Champion!

These mighty sporty superheroes are taking part in the **Trans-galaxy Superhero Games**! Their mission is to practise their times tables along the way, demonstrating mighty skills in multiplying, dividing, and solving word problems!

There is, however, one problem! A super villain named **Dennis the Demon Digit Demolisher** and his pet, **Lorraine the Loathsome Dragon**, have an evil plan to make a world without numbers!

Can you help the mighty superheroes work their way through each event and stop super villain **Dennis the Demon Digit Demolisher** from sabotaging the events?

You will have to be mightily clever, mightily quick and mightily resourceful!

*Good luck!*

# Superhero wrist watch - 3x table

Can you make your own superhero wrist watch for *Mighty Hypersonic Heather*'s 3x table? Complete the questions, then cut out and wear the wrist watch.

1 x 3 = 3
2 x 3 = 6
3 x ☐ = 9
4 x 3 = ☐
5 x ☐ = 15
6 x 3 = ☐
☐ x 3 = 21
☐ x 3 = 24
9 x 3 = 27
10 x 3 = ☐
11 x 3 = ☐
☐ x 3 = ☐

## Home Challenge

Ask an adult to throw a ball high in the air to you and shout a number between 1 and 12. Multiply the number by 3 as you catch it.

## Mighty Challenge

Can you write out your 3x table four times on a whiteboard? How long did it take you? Can you do it again, but quicker?

Mighty Fun Activities for Practising Times Tables, Book 2

# Hypersonic Heather's mask

15:00  3x

How did you do?

Can you finish *Mighty Hypersonic Heather*'s superhero mask by filling in the answers? Decorate the mask, but take care not to colour over the questions as you will lose your super powers!

1 x 3 =
3 ÷ 3 =

2 x 3 =
6 ÷ 3 =

3 x 3 =
9 ÷ 3 =

9 x 3 =
27 ÷ 3 =

4 x 3 =
12 ÷ 3 =

10 x 3 =
30 ÷ 3 =

5 x 3 =
15 ÷ 3 =

11 x 3 =
33 ÷ 3 =

6 x 3 =
18 ÷ 3 =

12 x 3 =
36 ÷ 3 =

7 x 3 =
21 ÷ 3 =

8 x 3 =
24 ÷ 3 =

## Home Challenge

Put sticky notes with numbers 1–12 on them high up on your wall. Go to the other side of the room. Run across, jump and grab a number. Multiply it by 3. How many can you answer in 2 minutes?

## Mighty Challenge

If there were 36 pairs of superhero goggles but they had to be shared equally between 3 races, how many where there for each one?

# Mighty high jump

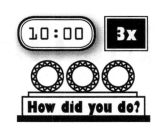
It's the most important jump of the day. *Mighty Hypersonic Heather* needs to jump high enough to reach and solve all the questions to win. Let's hope her cape makes her fly mighty high!

3 × 8 =

5 × 3 =

3 × 3 =

3 × 9 =

3 × 4 =

7 × 3 =

10 × 3 =

2 × 3 =

6 × 3 =

12 × 3 =

11 × 3 =

## Home Challenge

Get an adult to write some 3x table questions on cards and hang them on a washing line. Then jump and get them. How many can you answer?

## Mighty Challenge

Heather grabbed 3 cards in the first jump, 3 cards in the second jump and 3 again in the third jump. How many cards did she collect altogether?

*Mighty Fun Activities for Practising Times Tables, Book 2*

# Kit check

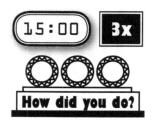
*Mighty Hypersonic Heather* likes to have 3x the amount of kit in her dressing room. Help work out how many of each item she has.

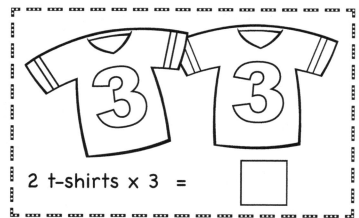

2 t-shirts x 3 = ☐

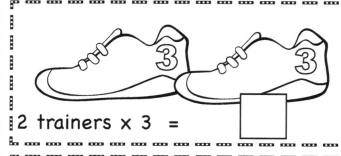

4 pairs of shorts x 3 = ☐

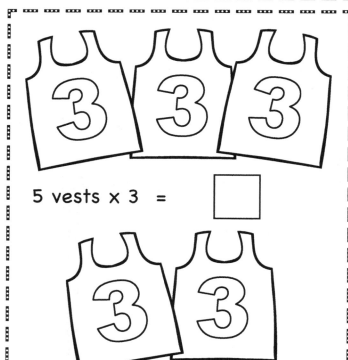

5 vests x 3 = ☐

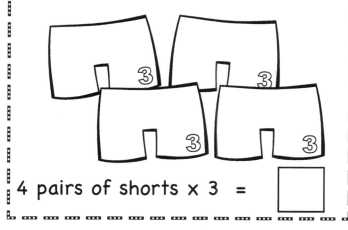

2 trainers x 3 = ☐

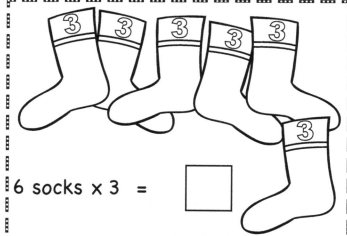

6 socks x 3 = ☐

## Home Challenge

Can you add up how many items you are wearing and times that number by 3?

## Mighty Challenge

Add some more items to *Mighty Hypersonic Heather's* wardrobe and then times them by 3.

# Blast the stars

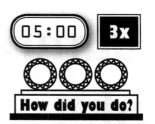

As part of superhero training, *Mighty Hypersonic Heather* must blast the stars with her number shooter and put a multiple of 3 on each star. Help her fill the stars with multiples of 3.

## Home Challenge

Visit a park. Run from one side of the park to the other, counting in 3s. How far can you get before getting tired?

## Mighty Challenge

Can you divide the number on each star by 3?

# Jump through the sky

*Mighty Hypersonic Heather* is jumping through the sky on a superhero mission. She needs to collect all the clouds that are multiples of 3. Colour them in to help her.

31

12

25

26

9

30

7

3

16

15

## Home Challenge

Hop and jump all the way to bed. On each move say a number that's a multiple of 3.

## Mighty Challenge

On each cloud write the number that is 3 more than the number shown.

# Complete the sequence

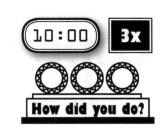

To earn superhero points, *Mighty Hypersonic Heather* must race against the clock to complete the sequences.

Mighty Fun Activities for Practising Times Tables, Book 2

# Cape challenge

During the event *Mighty Hypersonic Heather* has to give out mighty capes to all the teams. She has 33 capes to share between 3 teams. Can you draw the right amount of capes in each team's dressing room?

Superstars

The Wizards

Awesome Utd

## Home Challenge

Can you divide the washing pile equally between the number of people in your house mighty quick?

## Mighty Challenge

Can you write the above question as a number sentence?

# Trophy dash!

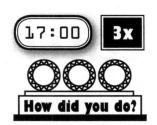

There is a mighty trophy to win in the event. However, *Dennis the Demon Digit Demolisher* has put some fire obstacles in the way. Luckily *Mighty Hypersonic Heather* is so good at jumping, that can she get over them, if she can answer the questions. Be quick! She has a time to beat of 17 minutes.

Finish

$30 \div 3 =$

$21 \div 3 =$

$18 \div 3 =$

$9 \div 3 =$

$3 \div 3 =$

$6 \div 3 =$

$27 \div 3 =$

$15 \div 3 =$

$36 \div 3 =$

$12 \div 3 =$

Start

## Home Challenge

Write some questions on card. Pretend they are hurdles on fire. Jump over them like a superhero, solving the problems.

## Mighty Challenge

Can you answer this mighty tricky question?
$48 \div 3 =$

# Catch the leaves!

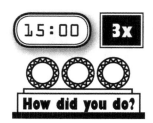

*Mighty Hypersonic Heather* needs to solve the number sentences on the leaves to gain superhero powers. Help her to jump up high! Can she beat *Dennis the Demon Digit Demolisher* who scored 8 correct answers? Watch out for Dennis who is blowing the leaves away!

## Home Challenge

Cut some leaf shapes out of paper and write questions on them. Then ask an adult to hold them high for you to jump up, grab a leaf and answer.

## Mighty Challenge

Add as many leaves to the picture as you can, featuring multiples of 3.

# Scoreboard code

**Crack the code to find the winner of round 1 of the super jump.**

A — 11
B — 42
C — 0
D — 9
E — 3
F — 101
G
H
I — 27
M
L — 39
K — 10
J — 53
N — 90
O — 93
P — 8
R — 4
S
12
36
6
T
Y
5
21
15

## Scoreboard

3x2=☐  9x3=☐  12x3=☐  36÷3=☐  15÷3=☐  3x7=☐

___  ___  ___  ___  ___  ___

4x3=☐  1x3=☐  33÷3=☐  15÷3=☐  3x4=☐  3x1=☐  12÷3=☐

___  ___  ___  ___  ___  ___  ___

## Home Challenge

Count the stars you can see tonight and times the number by 3. How many times can you jump whilst working out the answer?

## Mighty Challenge

Can you write questions to add the word HYPERSONIC to the scoreboard?

Mighty Fun Activities for Practising Times Tables, Book 2

# Results board

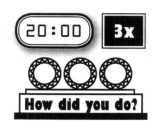

**Help *Mighty Hypersonic Heather* to work out her results to add to the score board.**

### Event 1
***Mighty Hypersonic Heather*** jumped 3 times in this event. In each jump she scored 7 points. How many points is this?

### Event 2
***Mighty Hypersonic Heather*** scored 12 points in each of her 3 jumps. How many is that for the 3 jumps combined?

### Event 3
Between 3 teammates they scored 24 points. They each scored the same, but only ***Mighty Hypersonic Heather*** can enter her results for this event. How many points did they each score?

### Event 4
***Mighty Hypersonic Heather*** had 2 friends in her team. They get to combine their scores in this event. They each score 5 points. How many did they score in total?

### Event 5
***Mighty Hypersonic Heather*** jumped 9 times and scored 3 points for each jump. How many altogether?

## RESULTS BOARD

| | |
|---|---|
| **EVENT 1** | points |
| **EVENT 2** | points |
| **EVENT 3** | points |
| **EVENT 4** | points |
| **EVENT 5** | points |

### Home Challenge
Jump around the house. Every time you see a door, count on in 3s.

### Mighty Challenge
If every jumper spent £3 entering the race and there was £18 in the pot, how many people entered?

# Superhero wrist watch - 4x table

Can you make your own superhero wrist watch for *Mighty Fishtail Freda*'s 4x table? Complete the questions, then cut out and wear the wrist watch.

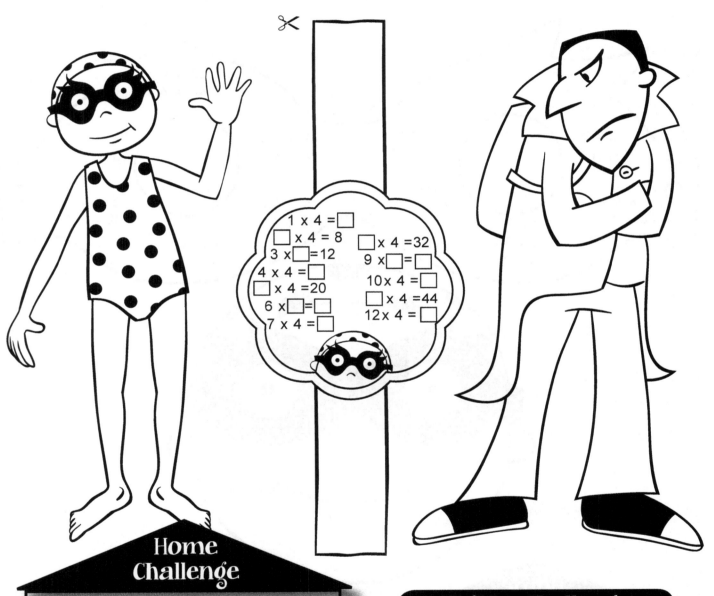

1 x 4 = ☐
☐ x 4 = 8
3 x ☐ = 12
4 x 4 = ☐
☐ x 4 = 20
6 x ☐ = ☐
7 x 4 = ☐
☐ x 4 = 32
9 x ☐ = ☐
10 x 4 = ☐
☐ x 4 = 44
12 x 4 = ☐

## Home Challenge

Next time you've having a bath, tip plastic numbers 1–12 into the bathtub. Swim down and pick them up one at a time. Multiply the number by 4. How many can you answer in 3 minutes?

## Mighty Challenge

Can you write one ÷ question for each of your answers? For example, 1 x 4 = 4 could be 4 ÷ 1 = 4 or 4 ÷ 4 = 1.

# Mighty Fishtail Freda's mask

How did you do?

Can you finish *Mighty Fishtail Freda*'s superhero mask by filling in the answers? Decorate the mask, but take care not to colour over the questions as you will lose your superpowers!

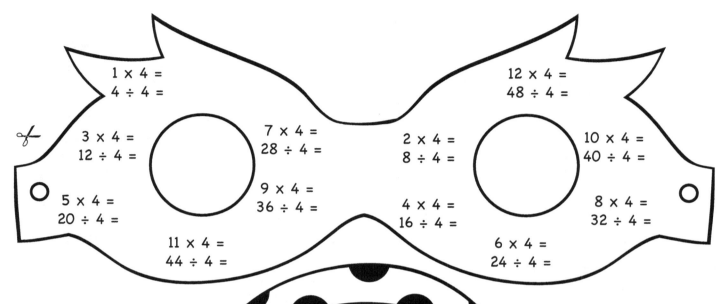

1 x 4 =
4 ÷ 4 =

12 x 4 =
48 ÷ 4 =

3 x 4 =
12 ÷ 4 =

7 x 4 =
28 ÷ 4 =

2 x 4 =
8 ÷ 4 =

10 x 4 =
40 ÷ 4 =

5 x 4 =
20 ÷ 4 =

9 x 4 =
36 ÷ 4 =

4 x 4 =
16 ÷ 4 =

8 x 4 =
32 ÷ 4 =

11 x 4 =
44 ÷ 4 =

6 x 4 =
24 ÷ 4 =

## Home Challenge

Cut out 12 fish from card and number them 1–12. Pretend to swim around the room. Every time you swim over a number, times it by 4.

## Mighty Challenge

Can you say how knowing your 2x table may help you to answer questions where you need to multiply by 4?

# Crack the password

**Dennis the Demon Digit Demolisher** has changed the entry password on the pool door to stop the competitors from swimming. Can you help *Mighty Fishtail Freda* to crack the password so the race can start on time?

3 x 4 = ☐ ____

4 x 4 = ☐ ____

1 x 4 = ☐ ____

4 x 3 = ☐ ____

8 x 4 = ☐ ____

6 x 4 = ☐ ____

7 x 4 = ☐ ____

2 x 4 = ☐ ____

8 x 4 = ☐ ____

5 x 4 = ☐ ____

4 = U
8 = I
12 = A
16 = Q
20 = H
24 = P
28 = L
32 = S
36 = T
40 = E
44 = R
48 = B

**Answer**

_ _ _ _ _ _ _ _ _ _ _ _ _

## Home Challenge

Next time you go swimming, can you count in 4s as you swim a length?

## Mighty Challenge

What other superpower could *Mighty Fishtail Freda* have? Can you write a new code and questions to match it?

Mighty Fun Activities for Practising Times Tables, Book 2

# Splash puddles!

**Dennis the Demon Digit Demolisher** has pushed *Mighty Fishtail Freda* into the pool and lost all of her multiples. Fill the splash puddles with multiples of 4 to help her get them back.

### Home Challenge

Jump in muddy puddles whilst shouting in 4s. How loud can you shout? (Don't forget your boots!)

### Mighty Challenge

Solve this problem and make a new splash puddle with the answer in it:
$$48 \div 4 =$$

# Pop the bubbles

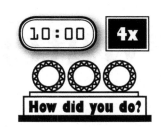

**10:00** **4x**

**How did you do?**

*Dennis the Demon Digit Demolisher* must pop bubbles with numbers that are not multiples of 4. Colour his bubbles black. *Mighty Fishtail Freda* has to pop bubbles that are multiples of 4. Colour hers red. Who has popped the most bubbles?

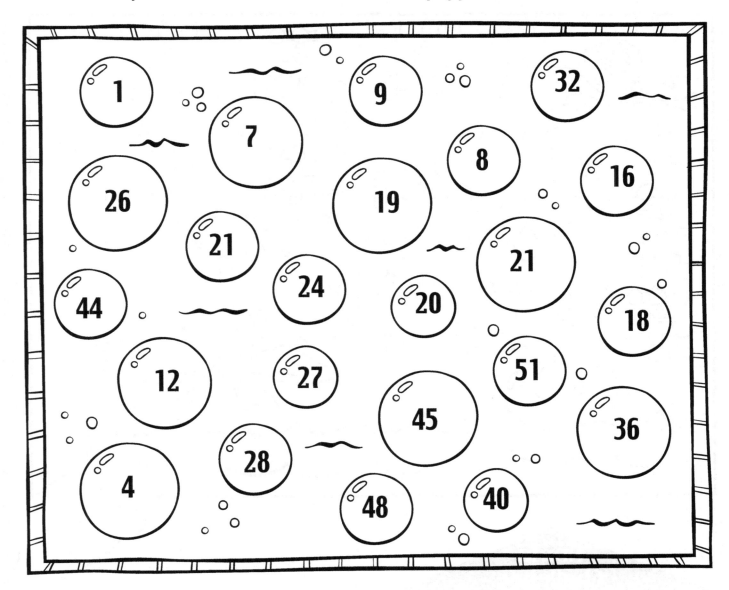

## Home Challenge

Blow some bubbles. Can you recite your 4x tables mighty quickly before they all pop?

## Mighty Challenge

Write a number sentence for 4 of the 4x table numbers in the pool. For example, 4 x 4 = **16.**

Mighty Fun Activities for Practising Times Tables, Book 2

# Water SOS!

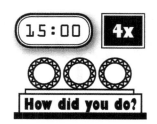
*Lorraine the Loathsome Dragon* has breathed holes into the side of the pool so the water is draining out! The only way to save the day is to pour 4x as much water into the pool as quickly as possible! Turn on all the taps by multiplying the numbers on the taps by 4.

## Home Challenge

Time how long your bath takes to fill. Can you multiply the number of minutes by 4? Can you time how long it takes other things to fill? Your sink? A can? A bucket?
Times the numbers by 4!

## Mighty Challenge

Can you see any numbers around you in your class? Can you multiply them by 4 and then by 4 again?

# Fix the bunting

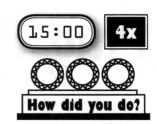
***Dennis the Demon Digit Demolisher*** has pulled down all the numbered flags on the swimming pool lanes. No one can race until they are put back. Help *Mighty Fishtail Freda* to cut out the flags and glue them back in the correct order. They go up in intervals of 4!

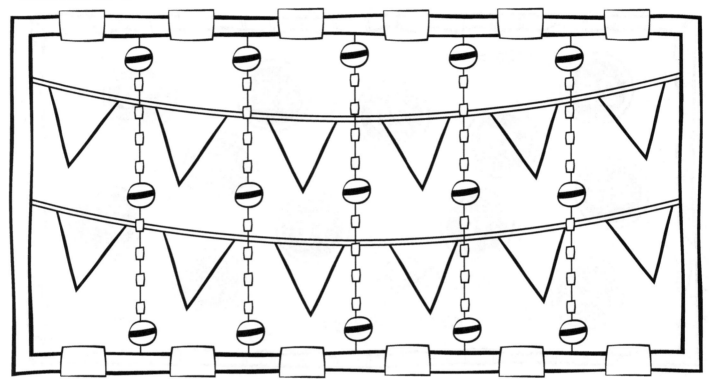

## Home Challenge

Can you make you own 4x table bunting and hang it in your bedroom? Get an adult to ask you questions and jump up at the answer!

## Mighty Challenge

Can you make the flag bunting longer, continuing to count in 4s?

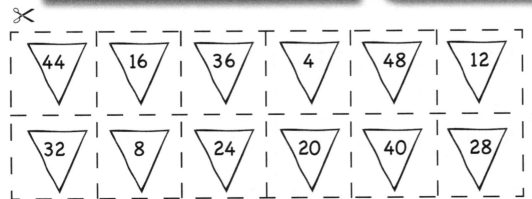

| 44 | 16 | 36 | 4 | 48 | 12 |
| 32 | 8 | 24 | 20 | 40 | 28 |

©Hannah Allum, Hannah Smart and Brilliant Publications

*Mighty Fun Activities for Practising Times Tables, Book 2*

# Plug the holes!

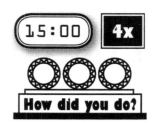

**15:00** **4x**

How did you do?

*Dennis the Demon Demolisher* has struck again. This time he has taken the plugs out of the swimming pool! *Mighty Fishtail Freda* has to divide the numbers on the holes at the bottom of the pool by 4 and stick the correct plug on!

## Home Challenge

How many times can you say your 4x table in the time your bath takes to run?

## Mighty Challenge

What number plug would you need to block a hole with 200 on it?

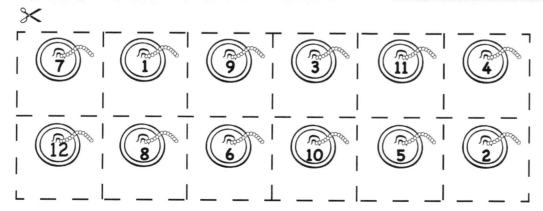

7  1  9  3  11  4

12  8  6  10  5  2

# The big race

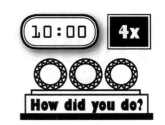

*Dennis the Demon Digit Demolisher* and *Mighty Fishtail Freda* are having a race to collect as many toys from the bottom of the pool as possible. Dennis collected and answered 6 questions in 10 minutes. Can you help Freda to beat this, to win the race?

$32 \div 4 =$

$40 \div 4 =$

$4 \div 4 =$

$16 \div 4 =$

$24 \div 4 =$

$48 \div 4 =$

$8 \div 4 =$

$20 \div 4 =$

$24 \div 4 =$

$44 \div 4 =$

$36 \div 4 =$

## Home Challenge

Write some questions on the bathroom tiles with soap. How quickly can you solve them?

## Mighty Challenge

Can you write word problems to match the answers on 4 of the questions?

Mighty Fun Activities for Practising Times Tables, Book 2

# Mighty fishtails!

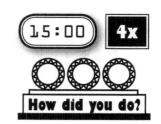
*Mighty Fishtail Freda* has a special superhero power. Her fishtail makes her swim mighty quick. Help her solve the problems on her different fishtails before *Dennis the Demon Digit Demolisher* drains the pool!

4 × 6

1 × 4

5 × 4

9 × 4

32 ÷ 4

28 ÷ 4

2 × 4

8 ÷ 4

48 ÷ 4

9 × 4

20 ÷ 4

### Home Challenge

Kick as fast as you can in the bath whilst saying your 4x table.

### Mighty Challenge

Add some more fishtails and write 4x table problems to solve on them.

# Locker codes

20:00  4x

How did you do?

**Dennis the Demon Digit Demolisher** has changed all the codes on the lockers.
Can you help *Mighty Fishtail Freda* to solve the questions and open the lockers by circling the answers.

3 x 4 =  | 3 | 1 | 4 | (1 | 2) |

24 ÷ 4 =  | 1 | 8 | (6) | 3 | 2 |

12 x 4 =  | 1 | 2 | (4 | 8) | 3 |

6 x 4 =  | (2 | 4) | 5 | 2 | 3 |

36 ÷ 4 =  | 6 | 5 | (9) | 1 | 8 |

10 x 4 =  | 0 | 4 | 8 | 0 | (4 | 0) |

44 ÷ 4 =  | 4 | 3 | (1 | 1) | 2 | 1 |

16 ÷ 4 =  | (2) | 5 | 4 | 8 | 7 |

4 x 7 =  | 2 | 6 | 2 | 5 | (2 | 8) |

4 x 4 =  | 5 | (1 | 6) | 3 | 7 |

8 x 4 =  | 1 | 8 | (3 | 2 | 6) |

7 x 4 =  | 2 | 6 | 2 | 8 | 1 | 5 |

48 ÷ 4 =  | 1 | 2 | 4 | 3 | 6 | 7 |

20 ÷ 4 =  | 5 | 6 | 9 | 1 | 4 | 3 |

9 x 4 =  | 2 | 1 | 3 | 2 | 3 | 6 |

32 ÷ 4 =  | 7 | 1 | 6 | 5 | 8 | 4 |

5 x 4 =  | 4 | 2 | 0 | 7 | 3 |

28 ÷ 4 =  | 5 | 4 | 6 | 7 | 2 |

12 ÷ 4 =  | 3 | 1 | 6 | 8 | 9 |

2 x 4 =  | (8 | 5 | 9 | 4) |

40 ÷ 4 =  | 1 | 0 | 0 | 1 | 8 |

8 ÷ 4 =  | 9 | 6 | 2 | 4 |

11 x 4 =  | 7 | 4 | 4 | 2 |

## Home Challenge

Can you remember this week to count in 4s every time you or someone in your family unlocks something (your house, a car, etc).

## Mighty Challenge

Can you think of 10 different 2 digit numbers that can be divided by 4?

©Hannah Allum, Hannah Smart and Brilliant Publications

*This page may be photocopied for use by the purchasing institution only.*

Mighty Fun Activities for Practising Times Tables, Book 2

# Word problems

**How did you do?**

**In order to earn a superhero mask, solve these word problems mighty quick.**

***Dennis the Demon Digit Demolisher*** has put 10 traps in each of the 4 lanes of the pool. How many traps are in the pool?

If there are 5 members of each team in a relay race and there are 7 teams, how many people are in the relay race?

***Dennis the Demon Digit Demolisher*** has stolen 48 floats. He shared them equally between 4 of his dragon friends. How many did each dragon get?

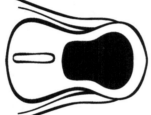

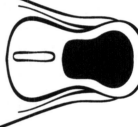

***Mighty Fishtail Freda*** has entered 8 races today. In each race she swims 4 lengths. How many lengths did she swim today in total?

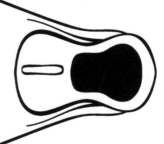

***Mighty Fishtail Freda*** trains 4 days a week. Each day she swims 12 lengths. How many lengths does Freda swim in training each week altogether?

## Home Challenge

Run 4 laps around your home. On each lap collect 4 items. How many items do you have at the end? Write a number sentence.

## Mighty Challenge

If each of the 12 superheroes gave £4 a week to swim in Freda's pool, how much would she make in a week?

# Superhero wrist watch - 6x table

Can you make your own superhero wrist watch for *Mighty Bubble Bursting Brenda*'s 6x table? Complete the questions, then cut out and wear the wrist watch.

1 x 6 = 6
2 x 6 = 12
3 x 6 = 18
4 x 6 = ☐
5 x 6 = 30
6 x 6 = 36
7 x 6 = ☐
8 x 6 = 48
9 x 6 = ☐
10 x 6 = 60
11 x 6 = 66
12 x 6 = 72

## Home Challenge

Get a pot of bubble mix. Every time you blow, count the numbers of bubbles and x6. Are you the quickest in your family?

## Mighty Challenge

Can you write mighty bubble bursting word problems for 11 x 6 and 8 x 6?

Mighty Fun Activities for Practising Times Tables, Book 2

# Bubble Bursting Brenda's mask

Can you finish *Mighty Bubble Bursting Brenda*'s superhero mask by filling in the answers? Decorate the mask, but take care not to colour over the questions as you will lose your superpowers!

1 x 6 =
6 ÷ 6 =

9 x 6 =
54 ÷ 6 =

3 x 6 =
18 ÷ 6 =

4 x 6 =
24 ÷ 6 =

11 x 6 =
66 ÷ 6 =

5 x 6 =
30 ÷ 6 =

6 x 6 =
36 ÷ 6 =

7 x 6 =
42 ÷ 6 =

2 x 6 =
12 ÷ 6 =

10 x 6 =
60 ÷ 6 =

12 x 6 =
72 ÷ 6 =

8 x 6 =
48 ÷ 6 =

## Home Challenge

Can you say your whole 6x table as you take giant steps from one side of the pool to the other?

## Mighty Challenge

Can you multiply or divide any different numbers by 6?

# Energy bubbles

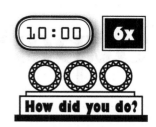

*Mighty Bubble Bursting Brenda* needs to dive down under the water and burst the bubbles to release a question. Help her solve all the questions so she'll get a mighty energy boost to help her beat the other superheroes.

6 x 5 =

7 x 6 =

6 x 1 =

6 x 8 =

6 x 6 =

6 x 4 =

12 x 6 =

2 x 6 =

11 x 6 =

6 x 3 =

## Home Challenge

Blow some bubbles. How many can you pop whilst counting in 6s to 72?

## Mighty Challenge

Two questions from the 6x table are missing. Can you add 2 extra bubbles with them on?

Mighty Fun Activities for Practising Times Tables, Book 2

# Super floats

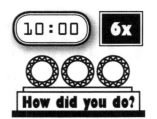

*Mighty Bubble Bursting Brenda* wants to beat *Dennis the Demon Digit Demolisher*! Help her to fetch numbers from the floats in the pool. Multiply each float by 6 and add the total to the scoreboard.

## Scorecard

| | |
|---|---|
| ___ × 6 = | ___ × 6 = |
| ___ × 6 = | ___ × 6 = |
| ___ × 6 = | ___ × 6 = |
| ___ × 6 = | ___ × 6 = |
| ___ × 6 = | ___ × 6 = |
| ___ × 6 = | ___ × 6 = |

## Home Challenge

Fill your bath or a bowl with a mighty large amount of bubbles. Get an adult to ask you 6x problems and write the answers in the bubbles with your finger.

## Mighty Challenge

What is the highest number you can score with 3 floats?

# Float chase

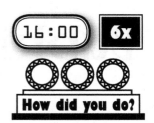
*Dennis the Demon Digit Demolisher* is chasing *Mighty Bubble Bursting Brenda*! Help her to race across the pool, stepping on floats! She can only step on the ones that are multiples of 6. Help her to find the path from the lowest to the highest number.

## Home Challenge

Pretend your room is a pool. Use sheets of paper as floats and write multiples of 6 on them. Can you cross the room, stepping only on floats?

## Mighty Challenge

Dennis put 6 x 15 deadly bubbles in the pool to stop Brenda! How many deadly bubbles were in the pool?

Mighty Fun Activities for Practising Times Tables, Book 2

# Bubble bursting

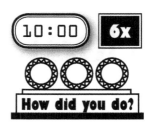
*Dennis the Demon Digit Demolisher* has sneakily filled the pool with frogs whilst the contestants weren't looking. Help *Mighty Bubble Bursting Brenda* by colouring in all the frogs that have a multiple of 6 on them.

## Home Challenge

Blow bubbles in your drink with a straw. How high in 6s can you count before they disappear?

## Mighty Challenge

For each 6x bubble, can you write a 6x number sentence. For example, 18:   3 x 6 = 18.

# Super goggles

The mighty sponsors have donated 66 pairs of superhero swim goggles. Can you share them between these 6 superhero swimmers?

Write the above question as a number sentence:

## Home Challenge

Sort all the bottles of shampoo etc in your bathroom into 6 piles. How many bottles are there in each pile?

## Mighty Challenge

If the sponsors added another 12 pairs of goggles to the pile, how many extra would each superhero get?

Mighty Fun Activities for Practising Times Tables, Book 2

# Diving for bubbles

**How did you do?**

Draw lines to match the superheroes to their bubble-tastic answer! Which superhero will find their bubble first?

$60 \div 6$   $36 \div 6$   $24 \div 6$   $12 \div 6$   $72 \div 6$   $30 \div 6$

## Home Challenge

Design a new swimsuit for Brenda with all the multiples of 6 on it.

## Mighty Challenge

Can you add more bubbles with multiples of 6 on them?

# Super diver

Help *Mighty Bubble Bursting Brenda* to crack the code to find the winner of the super dive competition.

| 2 x 6 | 66 ÷ 6 | 3 x 6 | 24 ÷ 6 | 1 x 6 | 18 ÷ 6 |
|-------|--------|-------|--------|-------|--------|
| 5 x 6 | 12 ÷ 6 | 6 x 5 | 5 x 6 | 6 x 4 | 30 ÷ 6 |
| 6 x 5 | 42 ÷ 6 | 5 x 6 | | | |

A 23
G 18
B 30
C 0
D 27
E 5
H 4
I 11
L 24
M 12
O 7
R 36
T 6
U 2
Y 3

**Answer**

_ _ _ _ _ _ _

_ _ _ _ _ _ _ _ _ _

## Home Challenge

Count backwards in 6s. When you reach 0, dive into the bath!

## Mighty Challenge

If you had 120 bubbles from 6 divers, how many did they blow each?

Mighty Fun Activities for Practising Times Tables, Book 2

# Underwater challenge

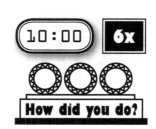

*Lorraine the Loathsome Dragon* is chasing *Mighty Bubble Bursting Brenda*. Brenda needs to stay underwater to avoid Lorraine's fire breath. Help her to burst the air bubbles by answering the questions on them so that she can stay underwater longer.

**Home Challenge**

How long can you blow bubbles in the bath for, whilst saying the 6x table in your head?

**Mighty Challenge**

Can you fill some more lanes with 6x table questions and solve them all?

# Underwater dive!

To win the race *Mighty Bubble Bursting Brenda* has to swim and collect superhero stars at the same time! Use a supercharged underwater pen to match the answers on the stars. Twist them around to write two x and two ÷ questions for each one!

$3 \times 6 = 18$
$6 \times 3 = 18$
$18 \div 3 = 6$
$18 \div 6 = 3$

**18  6  24  48  36  30  12  42**

## Home Challenge

How many times can you say your 6x table as you're running your bath?

## Mighty Challenge

Can you draw some more stars with higher multiples of 6 to get bonus points?

Mighty Fun Activities for Practising Times Tables, Book 2

# Superhero ducks

20:00 6x

**How did you do?**

*Mighty Bubble Bursting Brenda* has a disaster on her hands. The bubble answers on her mighty superhero ducks have floated away. Draw lines to join the ducks to the correct bubbles.

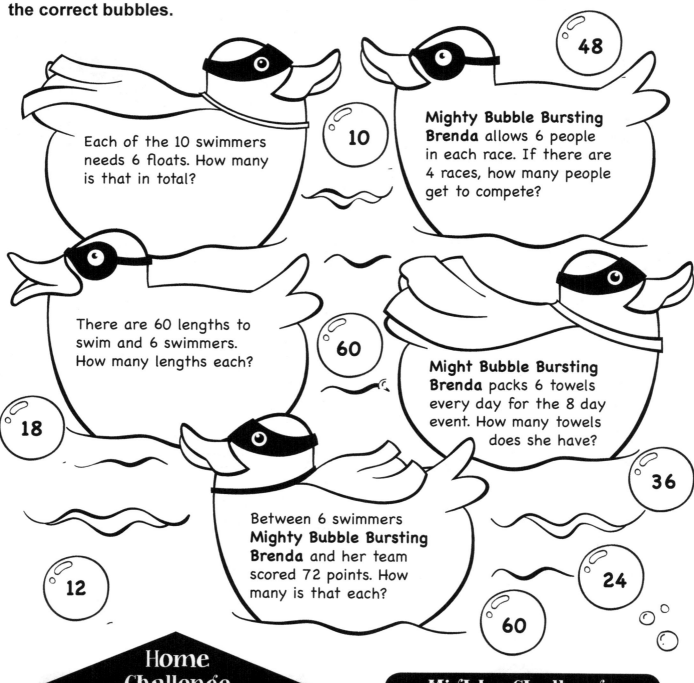

Each of the 10 swimmers needs 6 floats. How many is that in total?

10

**Mighty Bubble Bursting Brenda** allows 6 people in each race. If there are 4 races, how many people get to compete?

48

There are 60 lengths to swim and 6 swimmers. How many lengths each?

60

**Might Bubble Bursting Brenda** packs 6 towels every day for the 8 day event. How many towels does she have?

18

36

Between 6 swimmers **Mighty Bubble Bursting Brenda** and her team scored 72 points. How many is that each?

12

24

60

## Home Challenge

Walk to the park. When you get there, count the ducks in the pond (or other birds you see) in 6s.

## Mighty Challenge

Brenda scored 6 points in 9 races. ***Dennis the Demon Digit Demolisher*** scored 52 points in total. Who won?

# Superhero wrist watch - 8x table

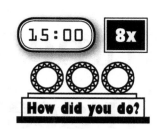

Can you make your own superhero wrist watch for *Mighty Time Traveller Tracey's* 8x table? Complete the questions, then cut out and wear the wrist watch.

1 x 8 = ☐          9 x 8 = ☐
☐ x 8 = ☐          ☐ x 8 = ☐
3 x ☐ = 24         ☐ x 8 = 88
4 x 8 = ☐          12 x 8 = ☐
☐ x 8 = 40
6 x ☐ = 48
7 x 8 = ☐
☐ x 8 = ☐

## Home Challenge

Go to a park and go on the swings. Each time your swing goes backwards count up in your 8x table!

## Mighty Challenge

Can you write your whole 8x table 5 times in 3 minutes? Is it correct?

Mighty Fun Activities for Practising Times Tables, Book 2

# Time Traveller Tracey's mask

Can you finish *Mighty Time Traveller Tracey*'s superhero mask by filling in the answers? Decorate the mask, but take care not to colour over the questions as you will lose your superpowers!

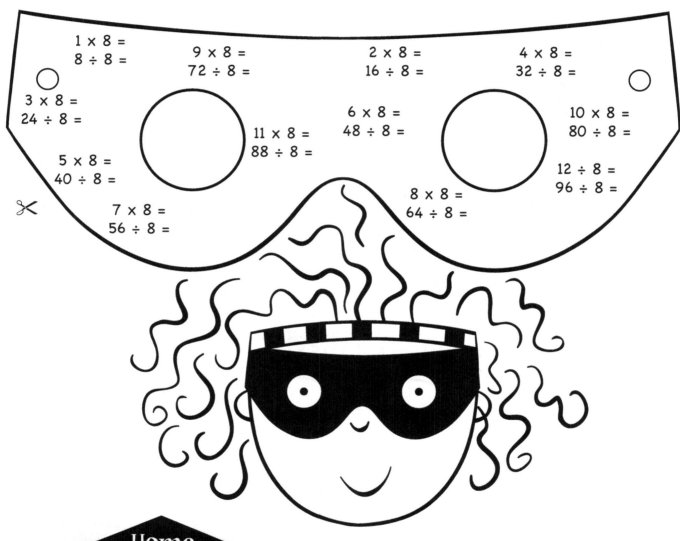

1 × 8 =
8 ÷ 8 =

9 × 8 =
72 ÷ 8 =

2 × 8 =
16 ÷ 8 =

4 × 8 =
32 ÷ 8 =

3 × 8 =
24 ÷ 8 =

6 × 8 =
48 ÷ 8 =

10 × 8 =
80 ÷ 8 =

11 × 8 =
88 ÷ 8 =

5 × 8 =
40 ÷ 8 =

12 ÷ 8 =
96 ÷ 8 =

8 × 8 =
64 ÷ 8 =

7 × 8 =
56 ÷ 8 =

## Home Challenge

Place 1–12 number cards inside a carrier bag. Shake them up and take one out at a time. Multiply each number by 8 as fast as you can whilst running on the spot. How many can you get correct in 1 minute?

## Mighty Challenge

Can you write *Mighty Time Traveller Tracey* word problems for 5 x 8 and 11 x 8?

# Jump to the stars

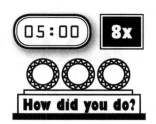

How far can you jump? Help *Mighty Time Traveller Tracey* to jump to the stars in the sandpit by writing an 8x table question to match the answers.

8    8 × ___ = ___

56    ___ × 8 = ___

16    ___ × 8 = ___

___ × 8 = ___    72

8 × ___ = ___    64

32    8 × ___ = ___

8 × ___ = ___    24

## Home Challenge

Cut out some stars and write some 8x questions on them. Fly or jump to them whilst saying the answers.

## Mighty Challenge

Can you add some more stars containing an answer in the 8x table?

Mighty Fun Activities for Practising Times Tables, Book 2

# Save the planet!

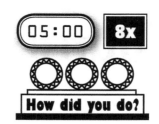

Help save Planet Mighty! *Dennis the Demon Digit Demolisher* is trying to blast Planet Mighty. *Mighty Time Traveller Tracey* needs to beat him there by jumping to each question and answering it correctly.

**Home Challenge**

Shout your 8x tables in your best 'alien' voice.

**Mighty Challenge**

Can you work out which 8x questions are missing from 1 x 8 up to 12 x 8? Draw some more stars and write the missing questions on them.

# Catch the capes

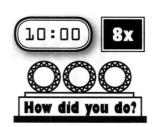

10:00  8x

How did you do?

*Dennis the Demon Digit Demolisher* has used a wind machine to blow *Mighty Time Traveller Tracey*'s capes away. Can you help her? Solve the questions on each of the masks and match them to the correct cape to help her get her super jumping powers back.

40  63  33  88

48  32  56

72  16  88  96

24

8 × 5 =

2 × 8 =

7 × 8 =

8 × 3 =

9 × 8 =

11 × 8 =

8 × 4 =   12 × 8 =   8 × 6 =

## Home Challenge

Can you recite your 8x tables backwards from 96 whilst jumping?

## Mighty Challenge

What is the highest number in the 8x table you can think of? What happens if you add 8?

Mighty Fun Activities for Practising Times Tables, Book 2

# Superhero race list

*Mighty Time Traveller Tracey* has to set up the race for 8 superheroes. Help her to complete her list of equipment she needs.

2 masks each _____

12 superpower energy
sweets each _____

6 racing obstacles each _____

9 bottles of water each _____

4 pairs of super socks each _____

10 flags each _____

## Home Challenge

Can you set up our own race at home for your family? You will need to make a list like Tracey's. Make sure it helps you to practise your 8x table.

## Mighty Challenge

Think of something else they will need for the race. How many do they need each? How many is that in total?

# Win the trophy!

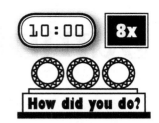
*Mighty Time Traveller Tracey* and *Dennis the Digit Demolisher* are racing to the trophy. Tracey has to find all the clouds that have multiples of 8 on them before Dennis. Don't let Dennis win! Colour the clouds when you find them.

## Home Challenge

Can you write an 8x table number sequence, starting from 16, in the air with your finger whilst hopping on the spot?

## Mighty Challenge

Add 8 to the numbers on all the clouds you have coloured in. How many of your new numbers are in the 8x table?

# Jumping blocks

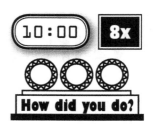

**Dennis the Demon Digit Demolisher** is causing trouble again. He has put three blocks in each of the sandpits so *Mighty Time Traveller Tracey* can't jump. Help Tracey to solve the problems, to knock the blocks over and be triumphant. Which jumping task will she solve quickest?

**Start**

32 ÷ 8 =

40 ÷ 8 =

64 ÷ 8 =

**Finish**

**Start**

80 ÷ 8 =

88 ÷ 8 =

96 ÷ 8 =

**Finish**

Jump Challenge Here!

**Start**

8 ÷ 8 =

16 ÷ 8 =

32 ÷ 8 =

**Finish**

**Start**

24 ÷ 8 =

48 ÷ 8 =

72 ÷ 8 =

**Finish**

## Home Challenge

Hop across the room saying your 8x table. Now hop backwards across the room, saying it backwards.

## Mighty Challenge

*Mighty Time Traveller Tracey* jumps in 32 events, taking 8 hours to do so. How many events does she do per hour?

# Crack the code

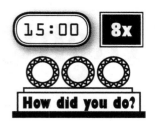

**Help crack the code on *Mighty Time Traveller Tracey*'s cape.**

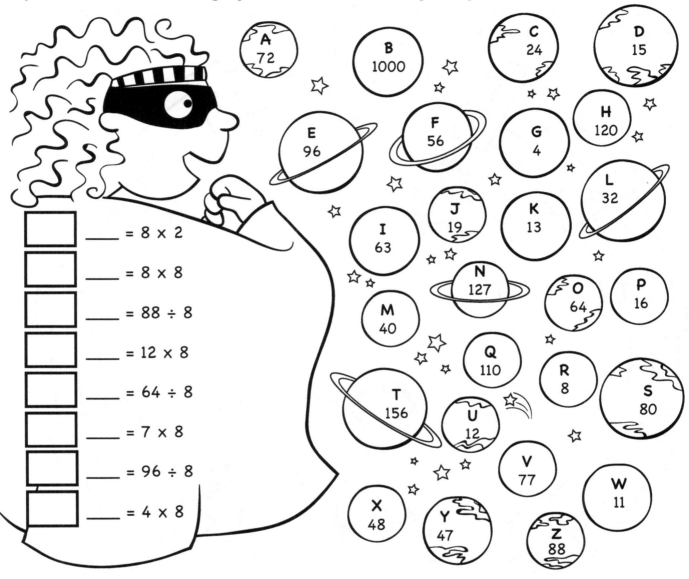

A 72
B 1000
C 24
D 15
E 96
F 56
G 4
H 120
I 63
J 19
K 13
L 32
M 40
N 127
O 64
P 16
Q 110
R 8
S 80
T 156
U 12
V 77
W 11
X 48
Y 47
Z 88

____ = 8 × 2

____ = 8 × 8

____ = 88 ÷ 8

____ = 12 × 8

____ = 64 ÷ 8

____ = 7 × 8

____ = 96 ÷ 8

____ = 4 × 8

**Answer**

___ ___ ___ ___ ___ ___ ___ ___

## Home Challenge

Design a planet that features all the multiples of 8 that you can think of.

## Mighty Challenge

Think of the highest number in the 8x table you can, then divide that number by 8. What's the answer?

Mighty Fun Activities for Practising Times Tables, Book 2

# Mighty challenge

Help *Mighty Time Traveller Tracey* to complete the race by answering the questions on all the jumps. She is racing against *Dennis the Demon Digit Demolisher,* so she needs to be mighty quick!

Start

Finish

8 × 4

64 ÷ 8

8 × 7

80 ÷ 8

4 × 8

96 ÷ 8

2 × 8

16 ÷ 8

40 ÷ 8

32 ÷ 8

8 ÷ 8

## Home Challenge

Write some 8x or ÷ 8 questions on cards. Place them on the ground in a circuit. See if you can jump over them whilst shouting the answers.

## Mighty Challenge

Get a friend to race you to answer the questions again. See if you can beat them by 8 seconds.

# Cape problems

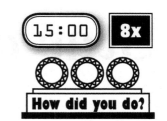

**How did you do?**

Solve the questions on *Mighty Time Traveller Tracey*'s capes.

Tracey notices 8 moons around each of the 8 planets she flew past today. How many is that altogether?

If each of the 8 contestants in the race gave Tracey £2 entry money, how much did she make altogether?

Tracey had 32 jumps to put out. How many jumps did each of the 8 contestants have to jump?

Each of the jumpers has 4 different super-powers. How many superpowers is that in total?

There are 64 entries to the mighty super race. Only 8 contestants can be in each race. How many races will there need to be?

## Home Challenge

Wear a cape and jump around the house firing 8x table questions at your friends and family. Make sure they get them mighty right!

## Mighty Challenge

There are 8 jumping contestants. Each needs 6 jumps and 4 flags. How many items are there to prepare?

Mighty Fun Activities for Practising Times Tables, Book 2

# Star questions

*Mighty Time Traveller Tracey* **is trying to get to Planet Jumptastic. In order to get there, she needs to complete the questions on the stars. Can you help?**

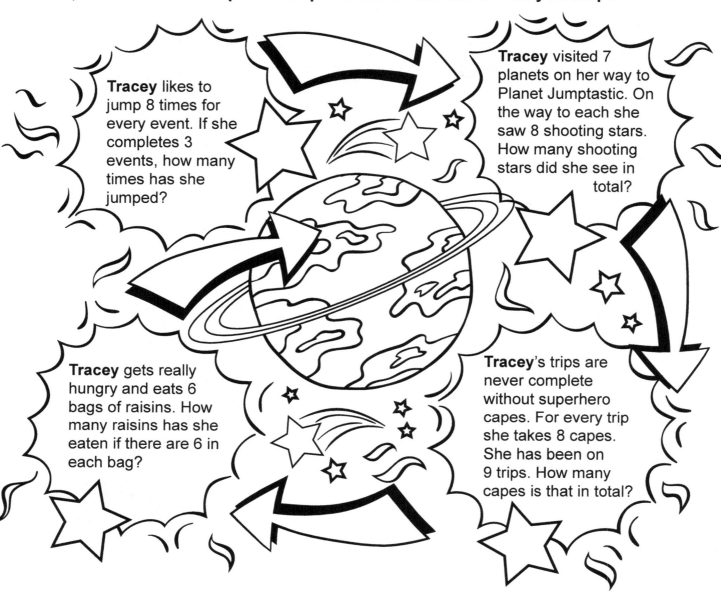

**Tracey** likes to jump 8 times for every event. If she completes 3 events, how many times has she jumped?

**Tracey** visited 7 planets on her way to Planet Jumptastic. On the way to each she saw 8 shooting stars. How many shooting stars did she see in total?

**Tracey** gets really hungry and eats 6 bags of raisins. How many raisins has she eaten if there are 6 in each bag?

**Tracey**'s trips are never complete without superhero capes. For every trip she takes 8 capes. She has been on 9 trips. How many capes is that in total?

## Home Challenge

Can you write your own 8x table word problem for **Tracey** to solve whilst flying around the room?

## Mighty Challenge

*Tracey's* cape has 8 green, 8 red, 8 yellow and 8 gold stars. How many stars are there in total?

# Mighty rockets at the ready!

*Dennis the Demon Digit Demolisher* has hidden sports equipment in the sky. Help the superheros to get it all back. Time how long it takes you to complete each sequence. Write your time on the rocket. The quickest superhero wins!

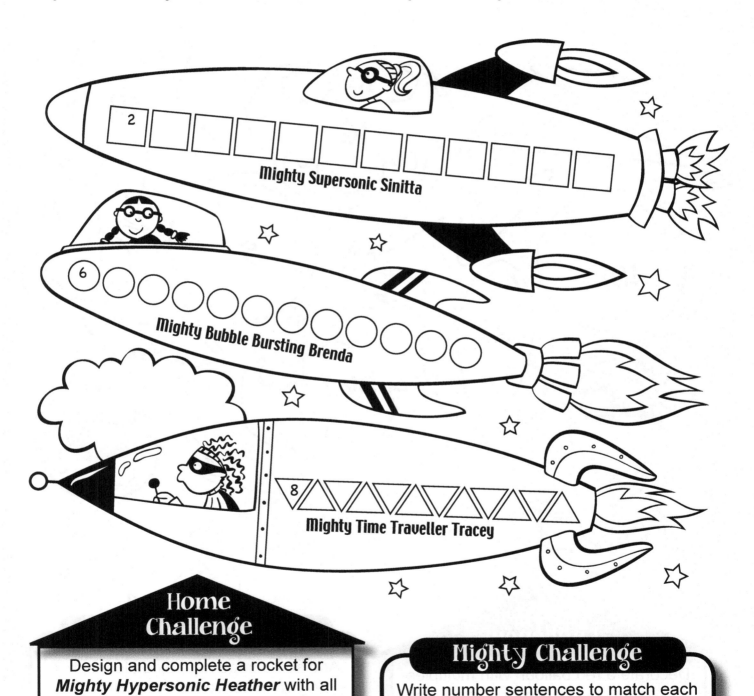

Mighty Supersonic Sinitta

2

Mighty Bubble Bursting Brenda

6

Mighty Time Traveller Tracey

8

## Home Challenge

Design and complete a rocket for *Mighty Hypersonic Heather* with all the 3s on it.

## Mighty Challenge

Write number sentences to match each multiple on one of the rockets.

*Mighty Fun Activities for Practising Times Tables, Book 2*

# Superhero balloon muddle

It's the day of the semi-finals. *Mighty Hypersonic Heather* is giving out red balloons to her mighty 3x supporters. *Mighty Fishtail Freda* is giving out blue 4x balloons. Colour the balloons the correct colours. Take care! Some balloons will need to be both colours!

## Home Challenge

Decorate a red balloon with multiples of 3 and a blue balloon with multiples of 4.

## Mighty Challenge

Add some superhero 8x balloons that *Mighty Bubble Bursting Brenda* would give out.

# Whose rocket?

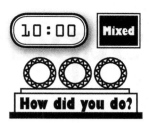
The superheroes are zooming into space to catch *Dennis the Demon Digit Demolisher*. Use the mulitples on each rocket to work out who is in each one. Draw a line to the character.

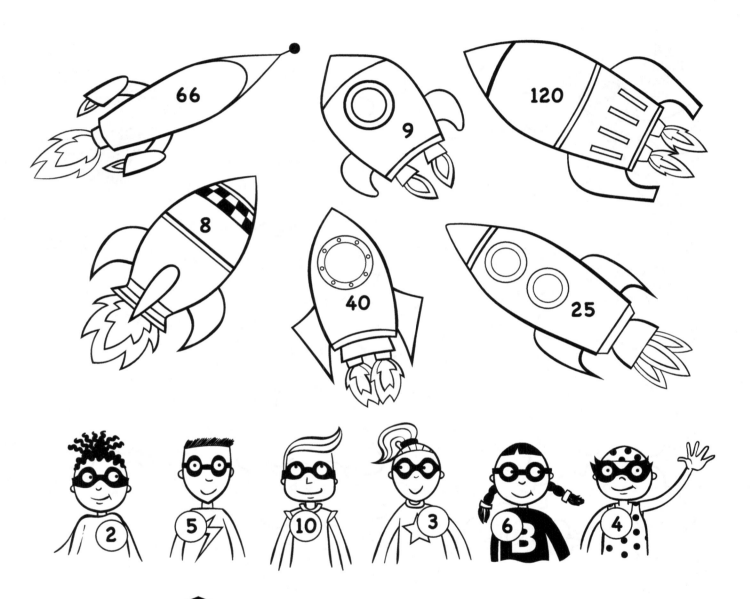

## Home Challenge

Fly around the house like a rocket saying your 6x table. Can you finish before an adult can count down from 10 to blast off?

## Mighty Challenge

Could any of the rockets belong to more than 1 character? Why?

Mighty Fun Activities for Practising Times Tables, Book 2

# Superhero race

*Mighty Fishtail Freda* and *Mighty Bubble Bursting Brenda* are having a race! They need to solve the problems, then join the clouds that are their multiples. Freda is going to start at 4 and count in 4s and Brenda is going to start at 6 and count in 6s.

**x4**
Mighty Fishtail Freda

**x6**
Mighty Bubble Bursting Brenda

$16 \div 4 =$

$36 \div 6 =$

$4 \times 2 =$

$2 \times 6 =$

$3 \times 4 =$

$6 \times 3 =$

$4 \times 4 =$

$6 \times 4 =$

$7 \times 4 =$

$4 \times 6 =$

$5 \times 4 =$

$5 \times 6 =$

$8 \times 4 =$

$7 \times 6 =$

$6 \times 6 =$

$8 \times 6 =$

$4 \times 9 =$

$6 \times 9 =$

$10 \times 6 =$

$4 \times 11 =$

$10 \times 4 =$

$6 \times 12 =$

$11 \times 6 =$

## Home Challenge

Can you find any multiples of 4 which are also multiples of 6?

## Mighty Challenge

$6 \times$ ___ is the same as $4 \times 6 =$ ___ . What division questions can be made with this question?

*Mighty Fun Activities for Practising Times Tables, Book 2*

# Trails of clouds

The rockets are leaving trails of clouds behind. Continue the number sequence on each. Whoever fills in the most numbers wins this mission.

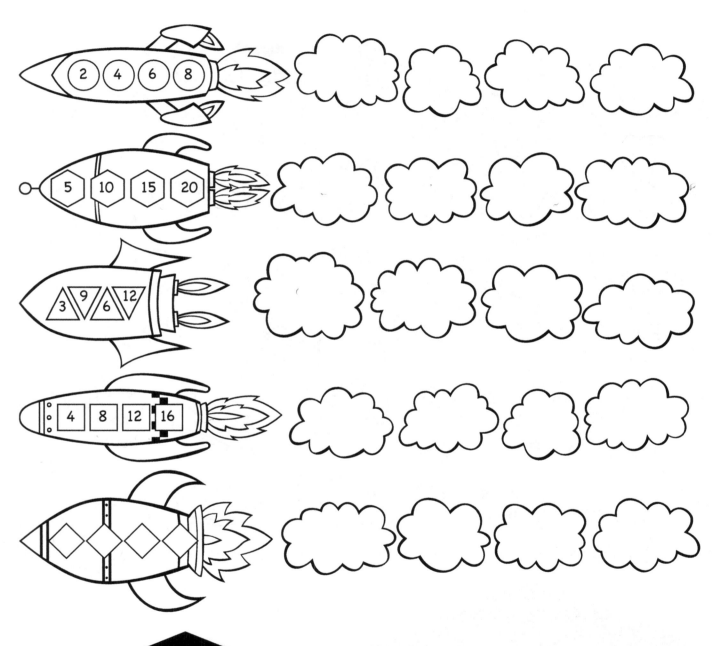

**Home Challenge**

Put some shaving foam in a tray. Use a finger to write the 4x table in it.

**Mighty Challenge**

Fill in the last rocket for the 6x table.

Mighty Fun Activities for Practising Times Tables, Book 2

# Trainer muddle!

*Lorraine the Loathsome Dragon* is breathing fire on to all the mighty numbered trainers! Can you save them by matching the pairs of trainers back together in time? Draw lines to join the pairs.

## Home Challenge

Imagine *Lorraine the Loathsome Dragon* is chasing you. Run around the house or garden. Get an adult to fire questions from the 3, 4, 6 and 8 times tables as you run.

## Mighty Challenge

Can you draw some trainer pairs for numbers not included on this page from the 3, 4, 6 and 8x tables?

# Obstacle course

Some of the mighty heroes are taking part in an obstacle course! They must multiply some numbers along the way Can you help them? Multiply all the numbers for each competitor.

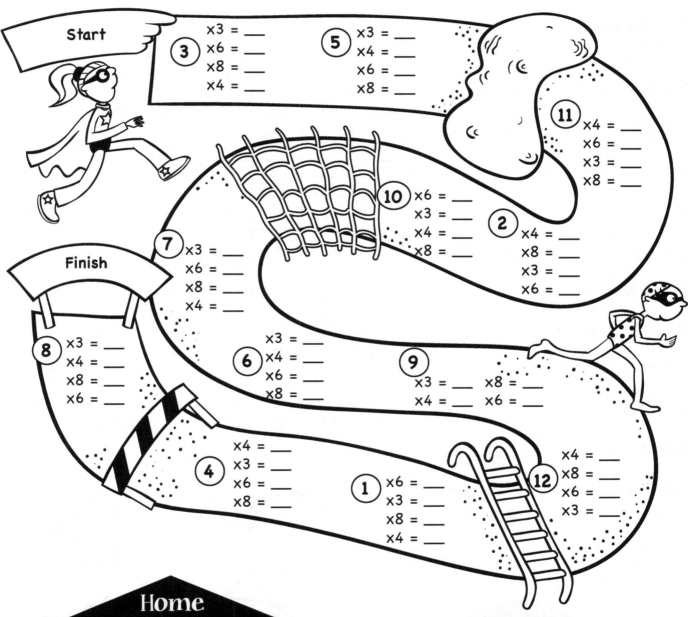

Start

3  x3 = __  x6 = __  x8 = __  x4 = __

5  x3 = __  x4 = __  x6 = __  x8 = __

11  x4 = __  x6 = __  x3 = __  x8 = __

10  x6 = __  x3 = __  x4 = __  x8 = __

2  x4 = __  x8 = __  x3 = __  x6 = __

7  x3 = __  x6 = __  x8 = __  x4 = __

Finish

6  x3 = __  x4 = __  x6 = __  x8 = __

9  x3 = __  x8 = __  x4 = __  x6 = __

8  x3 = __  x4 = __  x8 = __  x6 = __

4  x4 = __  x3 = __  x6 = __  x8 = __

1  x6 = __  x3 = __  x8 = __  x4 = __

12  x4 = __  x8 = __  x6 = __  x3 = __

## Home Challenge

Get an adult to shout out physical commands, such as run, hop, skip. While you are doing these, get them to shout out questions from the 3, 4, 6 and 8x tables.

## Mighty Challenge

Can you draw your own track? Write some numbers on it and try to answer them in less time than it took you to complete this track.

Mighty Fun Activities for Practising Times Tables, Book 2

# Co-ordinate rescue

*Dennis the Demon Digit Demolisher* **has rubbed out all the scores for the previous races. Can you read the co-ordinates, rescue the number score and write a question that matches it?**

For example:

Q1 (3,5)  12    3 × 4 = 12

Q2 (7,10) ☐ _____

Q3 (6,5) ☐ _____

Q4 (4,9) ☐ _____

Q5 (3,7) ☐ _____

Q6 (1,10) ☐ _____

Q7 (6,4) ☐ _____

Q8 (5,5) ☐ _____

Q9 (4,3) ☐ _____

Q10 (6,8) ☐ _____

Q11 (3,11) ☐ _____

Q12 (2,2) ☐ _____

| | 0 | 1 | 2 | 3 | 4 | 5 | 6 | 7 |
|---|---|---|---|---|---|---|---|---|
| 12 | 4 | 3 | 24 | 40 | 32 | 9 | 36 | 24 |
| 11 | 28 | 8 | 96 | 8 | 36 | 32 | 12 | 64 |
| 10 | 15 | 36 | 24 | 30 | 36 | 18 | 32 | 64 |
| 9 | 12 | 20 | 4 | 16 | 20 | 6 | 56 | 3 |
| 8 | 40 | 12 | 6 | 33 | 48 | 16 | 16 | 48 |
| 7 | 6 | 9 | 56 | 21 | 92 | 28 | 48 | 96 |
| 6 | 16 | 42 | 6 | 36 | 12 | 64 | 2 | 24 |
| 5 | 15 | 9 | 8 | 12 | 72 | 56 | 42 | 12 |
| 4 | 15 | 48 | 21 | 4 | 18 | 44 | 72 | 88 |
| 3 | 18 | 30 | 8 | 72 | 6 | 24 | 54 | 40 |
| 2 | 27 | 12 | 88 | 80 | 12 | 60 | 80 | 20 |
| 1 | 24 | 66 | 15 | 32 | 30 | 72 | 16 | 88 |

Read the co-ordinates across, then up.

## Home Challenge

Hide multiples from the 3, 4, 6 and 8x tables around the house. Race your family to find them and then shout out questions to go with the answers.

## Mighty Challenge

Pick some different co-ordinates. Write questions to match.

# Snack time

All the competitors need snacks and drinks for the races, but *Dennis the Demon Digit Demolisher* has sent his pet *Lorraine the Loathsome Dragon* to gobble them all up! Can you help to work out how many new ones to buy? Multiply the food and drink to work out how many are needed!

**8**

4 lots _____
6 lots _____
8 lots _____
3 lots _____

**5**

4 lots _____
8 lots _____
6 lots _____
3 lots _____

**9**

3 lots _____
6 lots _____
8 lots _____
4 lots _____

**11**

3 lots _____
4 lots _____
6 lots _____
8 lots _____

You find some snacks in the sports locker but there will not be enough. Use division to see how many each competitor can have.

64 bananas between 8 runners?  _____ each

44 orange juices between 4 swimmers?  _____ each

42 energy cubes between 6 high jumpers?  _____ each

18 bottles of squash between 3 cyclists?  _____ each

## Home Challenge

Next time you go to the shops, look in your basket. Imagine if you had to buy enough for 4 people. How many of each item would now be in your basket?

## Mighty Challenge

Can you share 100 chocolate medals between 4 competitors?

# Scoop the planets

**Dennis the Demon Digit Demolisher** has sent all the competitors' scores into space! Can you cut out the planets and stars at the bottom of the page and put them into the correct nets, so that the mighty superheroes can scoop them up? Be quick before Dennis catches you!

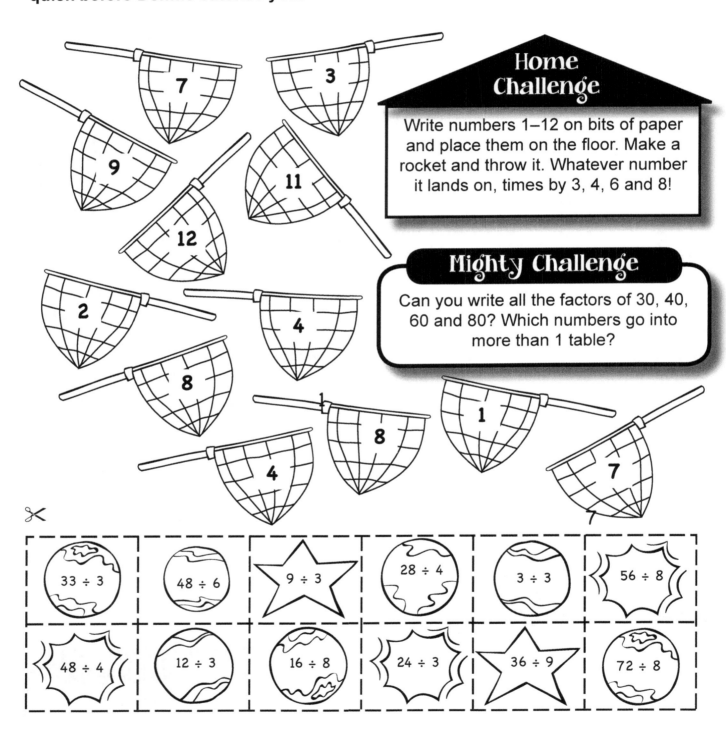

### Home Challenge

Write numbers 1–12 on bits of paper and place them on the floor. Make a rocket and throw it. Whatever number it lands on, times by 3, 4, 6 and 8!

### Mighty Challenge

Can you write all the factors of 30, 40, 60 and 80? Which numbers go into more than 1 table?

Nets: 7, 3, 9, 11, 12, 2, 4, 8, 8, 4, 1, 7

Cards: 33 ÷ 3, 48 ÷ 6, 9 ÷ 3, 28 ÷ 4, 3 ÷ 3, 56 ÷ 8, 48 ÷ 4, 12 ÷ 3, 16 ÷ 8, 24 ÷ 3, 36 ÷ 9, 72 ÷ 8

# Answers to code sheets

**Scoreboard code**     **page 16**
Mighty Heather

**Crack the password**     **page 21**
Aquasplish

**Super diver**     **page 39**
Mighty Bubble Bob

**Crack the code**     **page 51**
Powerful

Lightning Source UK Ltd.
Milton Keynes UK
UKOW07f1330030117
291295UK00001B/10/P

9 781783 172689